Successful Co-Parenting with a Toxic Ex

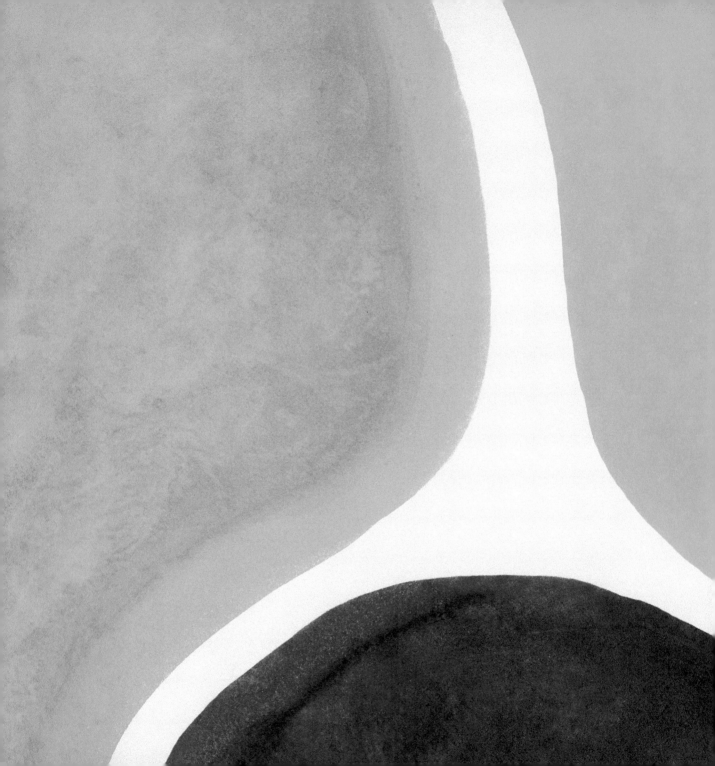

Successful Co-Parenting
with a Toxic Ex

A Guided Journal to Support and
Encourage You and Your Children

Susan Buniva, MSW

ROCKRIDGE
PRESS

For general information on our other products and services or to obtain technical support, please contact our Customer Care Department within the United States at (866) 744-2665, or outside the United States at (510) 253-0500.

Rockridge Press publishes its books in a variety of electronic and print formats. Some content that appears in print may not be available in electronic books, and vice versa.

Interior and Cover Designer: Jenny Paredes
Art Producer: Janice Ackerman
Editor: Jed Bickman
Production Editor: Sigi Nacson
Production Manager: Riley Hoffman

Illustration: © 2021 Callahan/Shutterstock
Author Photo Courtesy of Page Dowdy

Paperback ISBN: 978-1-63807-946-0
R0

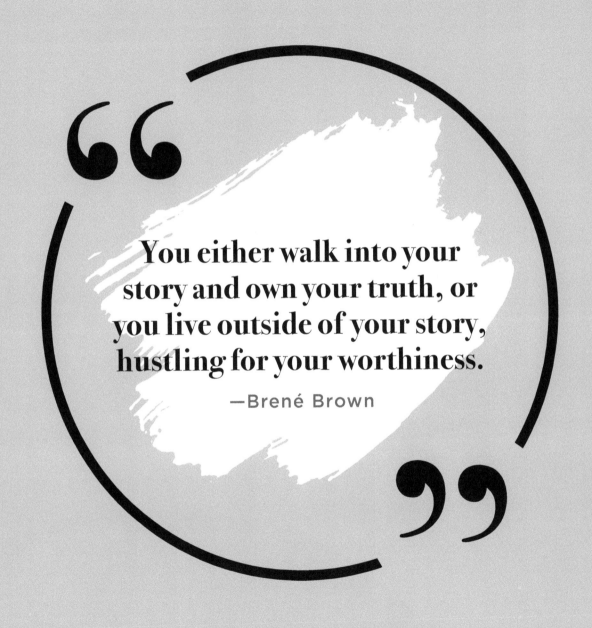

"You either walk into your story and own your truth, or you live outside of your story, hustling for your worthiness.

—Brené Brown

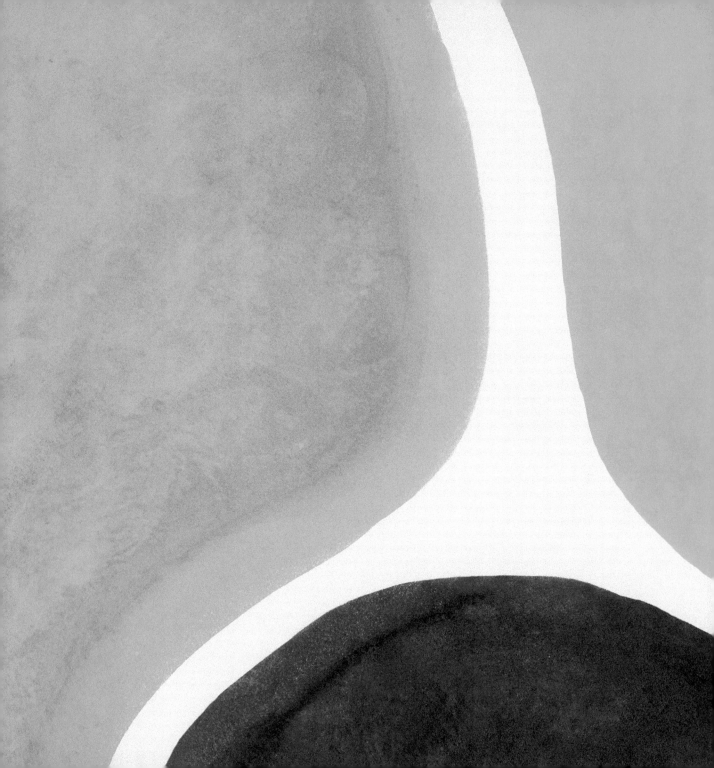

CONTENTS

INTRODUCTION

Welcome. I am so glad you are here. You are going through an incredibly challenging time and need some support. I want to be that support for you. I am not just a therapist, divorce coach, and co-parent counselor; I am also someone who has been through a difficult divorce. It was only after my divorce, my own mistakes, and almost 30 years of clinical experience that I realized there had to be a better way and went to get more training. After that formal training, much of my practice shifted to working with individuals and families struggling with these issues. The rest of my training came from individuals and families who opened their hearts and shared their struggles and insights. As a result, I was able to find meaning and growth in a horrible experience, and help others do the same. I hope this journal will be your safe place to heal and find your own growth and meaning.

Of course, no one goes into a relationship imagining it will fall apart. But to have it in fact fall apart, and then be forced to continue working in that problematic relationship as co-parents, can feel like a death sentence. If one set out to design a more challenging interpersonal situation, it would be hard to top this scenario. So, I have created this book to help you make peace with what brought you to this place, learn how to co-parent in a way that best serves your children, help your child through the transition, and ultimately heal the wounds within you.

This journal will not give you three easy strategies for every situation. Instead, it will accompany you on this journey while recognizing and honoring your inner wisdom. This journal offers prompts and practices to help you consider the questions that will guide you to your inner knowing. When you bring compassion to yourself, accept your co-parent's wounds and limitations, and bring love to the process, you will be able to access universal wisdom that will allow you to co-parent effectively.

As you do so, you will learn you will have to let lies go uncorrected to keep your children out of the middle, stuck trying to figure out who is telling the truth. Your children need to be children. You will learn how to come to terms with the fact that you cannot control most of your co-parent's behavior and that your children have resilience and will learn to use the coping skills you have given them to manage less-than-ideal circumstances. It won't be easy, and it will require some painful moments of self-reflection. Finally, you will discover that divorce is not about justice but about peace.

By definition, having purchased this journal, you are interested in learning, self-reflection, and growth. You are someone who wants more than formulaic answers. You want to understand your role and do what you can, while understanding what isn't yours to do and what therefore must be released. You are someone who wants to do the inner work to remove the obstacles to healing that will allow you to approach your co-parent with respect and less angst. I'm even guessing that you're someone who has done the hard work of self-reflection before and reaped the rewards. May this journal support you in being your best self—and a parent you can be proud of—in your co-parenting journey.

HOW TO USE THIS JOURNAL

This journal is designed for you to use at your own pace. Allow this journal to be your safe place to come and retreat to when you are feeling overwhelmed, confused, exhausted, angry, or sad. Perhaps writing in this journal can feel like an invitation to return to your center. It is likely to be most effective if you do the reading and exercises in the order presented. Take your time rather than trying to complete it all at once, though. It is helpful to have time to reflect on issues of this magnitude.

Before you respond to a prompt or a practice, make sure you are in a private, quiet place. You may want to light a candle, take a bubble bath, or make a soothing cup of tea. It is essential to perform small acts of kindness that internalize the message that you are worth the caring and compassion.

Many of the prompts invite a shift in thinking. Any time we are asked to shift our thinking or change a paradigm, we unconsciously try to protect ourselves from the perceived danger of entering the unknown. Notice how the "yes, but"s or the "but this is different" thoughts arise. What do these reactions stem from? Allow yourself to notice the feelings of anger and underlying fear and sadness. You don't have to change your thoughts or feelings. You just have to be present and compassionate with yourself. You have been through a lot, and the pain and frustration often persist as you work to find ways to co-parent in relative peace.

When you journal, try to approach the activity like a scientist collecting data. There is no bad data, no right or wrong. Everything is information without judgment. So, when we notice ourselves making judgments, that, too, is information. It's a clue about where we are stuck and what part of us needs healing and love. Without that healing, we cannot bring our best selves to the moment, and we become constricted, anxious, and depressed.

Guided journaling is a creative way to get to know yourself more deeply, create healing, and consider new ideas. Although it can have a therapeutic effect, it is not a substitute for therapy. Significant feelings of depression should be addressed with the help of a mental health professional. Individual therapy is always an option, and don't be shy about meeting with a few therapists to find the one who feels like a good fit for you.

Finally, it is essential to remember that journaling is not a grammar exercise or a call for a well-thought-through writing sample. Journaling is more about allowing an unfiltered stream of consciousness that helps us access the deeper feelings and associated thoughts we may not be aware of in our daily lives.

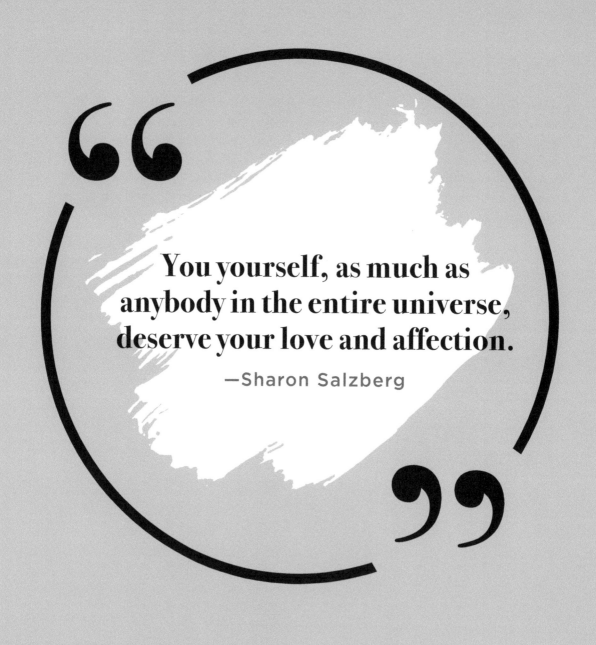

You yourself, as much as anybody in the entire universe, deserve your love and affection.

—Sharon Salzberg

Accepting Where You Are

ENDING YOUR MARITAL relationship and starting the journey toward a good co-parenting relationship is a challenging time of transition. We have to stop, take a deep breath, and see where we are, grieving the world we are leaving. Next, we will gently leave behind the dreams we had for our marriage with deep compassion, as well as the burden of trying to change our partner. We then have to assess both the wounds that need healing and the strengths that are emerging. Finally, it's time to forgive ourselves and our partners for the role we each played in the dissolution of the marriage—we do this for our children and for ourselves. It is hard to say which forgiveness process is more challenging, so be gentle and nurturing with yourself as you strive to do both. As you do, you can release the baggage of guilt, regret, resentment, and anger.

Now is the time to clean out the emotional closet, getting rid of self-doubt, tending to exhaustion, letting go of the worn-out anger and the tight expectations. Instead, it is time to tap into the inner strength you may have forgotten in the back of the closet, the ability to be your best self, and ultimately, the sense of adventure and anticipation for what awaits. So much of what we stashed in the closet was parts of ourselves that we lost and forgot about as we struggled in the marriage, feeling worn down and giving up pieces of who we were just to survive. This section is about remembering who we are and recognizing the potential of who we are becoming with deeper wisdom and healing.

What have I learned about myself in the marriage that will help me move forward in my life, particularly in my co-parenting relationship?

_____

_____

_____

_____

_____

_____

_____

_____

_____

_____

_____

_____

_____

_____

_____

As you begin this transition, you will often get triggered by your co-parent. It will take time before you have the detachment to be less vulnerable. When you feel triggered, this is a reminder to stop and take care of yourself.

1. Take a deep cleansing breath to the count of four, placing a gentle hand on your heart.

2. Pause to the count of four.

3. Slowly exhale to the count of eight, allowing yourself to let go of the stress.

4. Try it a few times now, and notice how relaxing this practice is.

What were the ways I felt unheard in my marriage? How might I communicate more effectively as a co-parent, to decrease defensiveness and increase the odds of being heard?

_____

_____

_____

_____

_____

_____

_____

_____

_____

_____

_____

_____

_____

_____

The enduring struggles in my marriage have taught me how strong I am. I will use that strength to let go of the marriage and bring my best self to the job of co-parenting.

My co-parent felt toxic to me in the marriage, but we are moving into a different relation-ship. What can I acknowledge about their strengths as a parent?

_____

_____

_____

_____

_____

_____

_____

_____

_____

_____

_____

_____

_____

_____

I now clearly see what was broken in my partner. I, too, have broken places that need healing. With love, I name those hurting places.

_____

_____

_____

_____

_____

_____

_____

_____

_____

_____

_____

_____

_____

When my co-parent triggers me, I want to go deeper and compassionately understand the wound that has been touched so that I can heal. What has been touched?

_____

_____

_____

_____

_____

_____

_____

_____

_____

_____

_____

_____

_____

_____

_____

_____

_____

_____

_____

_____

_____

_____

_____

_____

_____

_____

_____

_____

_____

_____

_____

_____

_____

In early co-parenting, there may still be much grief about the loss of the marriage. We must invite the feelings in, honoring any pain rather than distracting ourselves. Try to notice and validate these feelings before moving on. It is likely that there will be sadness, anger, guilt, or shame. Each emotion has a safe place inside you. We don't have to change the experience; just be with it. Pause and be aware of how profound this end is—if not for you, for the children—and how healing it can be simply to allow the feelings with curiosity and kindness and without judgment.

Some emotions keep coming up. But if I listen with kindness, I know my feelings need me to understand without judgment. If I understood my feelings, what might be different?

_____

_____

_____

_____

_____

_____

_____

_____

_____

_____

_____

_____

_____

_____

_____

Anger is a form of self-protection. So, what am I afraid of? Are there other ways I might protect myself that would bring me greater peace?

_____

_____

_____

_____

_____

_____

_____

_____

_____

_____

_____

_____

_____

_____

_____

I am learning I have the strength to let go of the hot coals of anger that are only burning my hands. I can do anything for my children and my healing. My growth feels good, and I am strong.

Now that I have survived a difficult divorce, what are the inner strengths I remember? How can I use these strengths to co-parent successfully and meet my own needs?

_____

_____

_____

_____

_____

_____

_____

_____

_____

_____

_____

_____

_____

_____

As I grow into this co-parenting relationship, what am I modeling for my children about relationships? What am I teaching them about respect, kindness, and communication? How do they see me?

_____

_____

_____

_____

_____

_____

_____

_____

_____

_____

_____

_____

_____

_____

_____

_____

_____

_____

_____

_____

_____

_____

_____

_____

_____

_____

_____

_____

_____

_____

_____

_____

When my children hear me talk about their co-parent, how can they tell I respect their co-parent and want them to have a good relationship with both of us?

_____

_____

_____

_____

_____

_____

_____

_____

_____

_____

_____

_____

_____

_____

_____

_____

_____

_____

_____

_____

_____

_____

_____

_____

_____

_____

_____

_____

_____

_____

_____

_____

_____

_____

_____

_____

Turn your wounds into wisdom.

—Oprah Winfrey

What goals do I have for myself as a parent and a growing human being while moving through this process? What might my gradual progress look like to me?

_____

_____

_____

_____

_____

_____

_____

_____

_____

_____

_____

_____

_____

_____

Separation, divorce, and co-parenting are exhausting journeys. I am tired, so how am I recharging my mind, body, and soul? Are there new things I want to do for myself?

_____

_____

_____

_____

_____

_____

_____

_____

_____

_____

_____

_____

_____

Write a list of all the negative judgments you make about yourself. It's probably a long list—we are often harder on ourselves than we would ever be on other people. When you have finished the list, make a statement responding to each of those things as a loving friend would. What might that friend help you understand about your history, your older wounds, and the perils of being human? Where did you learn to be so hard on yourself? Are you ready to grieve that and be more accepting of yourself?

How can I sort out leftover concerns about how I felt in the marriage from fears related to the children, to avoid projecting my feelings on to them? Clarifying this distinction is challenging but imperative.

_____

_____

_____

_____

_____

_____

_____

_____

_____

_____

_____

_____

_____

Co-parenting is a task that requires ongoing self-compassion and care. It is essential to be intentional about making choices to do nurturing things for yourself. Sometimes when we are most stressed, we can't even remember what might be soothing. Make a list of options you can carry with you at all times if you need a quick refresh. It might be as simple as taking a bubble bath, spending time with friends, practicing deep breathing, or buying a new kind of tea to savor or book to read by a favorite author. When you are kind to yourself, your children will benefit.

When self-care is not enough and we're running on fumes, we may need help from others. Is it a burden or honor when others ask for our support?

_____

_____

_____

_____

_____

_____

_____

_____

_____

_____

_____

_____

_____

_____

_____

How am I learning to trust and let others into my world? Can I trust that others love me and want to be there for me, growing closer in the process?

_____

_____

_____

_____

_____

_____

_____

_____

_____

_____

_____

_____

_____

_____

Although there is much I leave behind, I possess strengths and gifts nobody can take away. How can I use these assets to inform my co-parenting?

_____

_____

_____

_____

_____

_____

_____

_____

_____

_____

_____

_____

_____

_____

Co-parenting is as much about letting go of your marriage as it is about establishing a new and more distanced relationship. The marital problems will not be fixed but must be left behind. On scraps of paper, write down the unsolved marital issues, unfulfilled dreams, ways in which you wanted your former partner to change, things you wish you had done differently, and ways in which you wanted them to see you more accurately. Put the papers in a cardboard box and burn the collection in a bonfire or place them on a fireproof plate and carefully burn them. You may also rip them up or run them through a paper shredder. Allow these things to leave your heart as the smoke exits the sky.

Moving from a troubled marital relationship to an effective co-parenting relationship is a substantial shift that I am working to make with grace. The shift isn't always smooth, but it is one to be celebrated. I am a good parent.

I want to be aware of those things I am ready to let go of in my co-parent's parenting style. How will I let them parent differently than I parent?

_____

_____

_____

_____

_____

_____

_____

_____

_____

_____

_____

_____

_____

_____

Marriage is not about right and wrong. It is about two people dancing with each other. Each person's steps influence the steps their partner will take. With distance, it is easier to step back and wisely view the choreography. It becomes less about assigning blame and more about learning and moving forward. How can you be alert to the steps of that dance getting replicated in your co-parenting and step away to create a new dance as needed? When you notice old feelings arising, it may be your clue that you have an opportunity to identify those old dances and change them.

How would I explain the difference between being a partner and being a co-parent to a newly separated friend? What would be most helpful for them to know and deeply understand?

_____

_____

_____

_____

_____

_____

_____

_____

_____

_____

_____

_____

_____

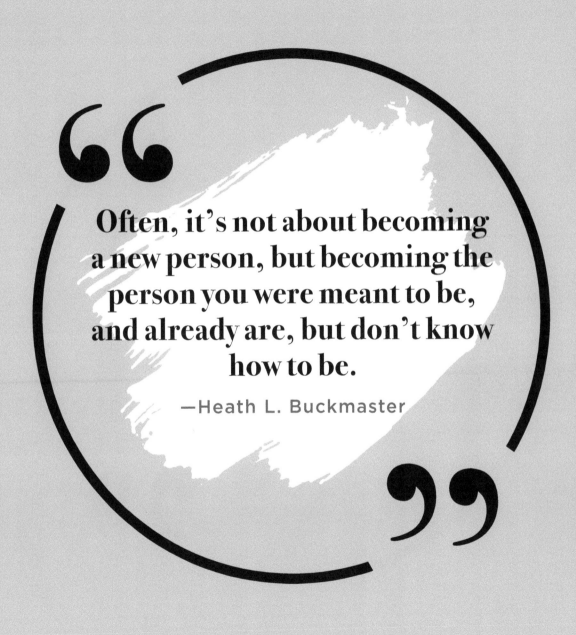

> Often, it's not about becoming a new person, but becoming the person you were meant to be, and already are, but don't know how to be.
>
> —Heath L. Buckmaster

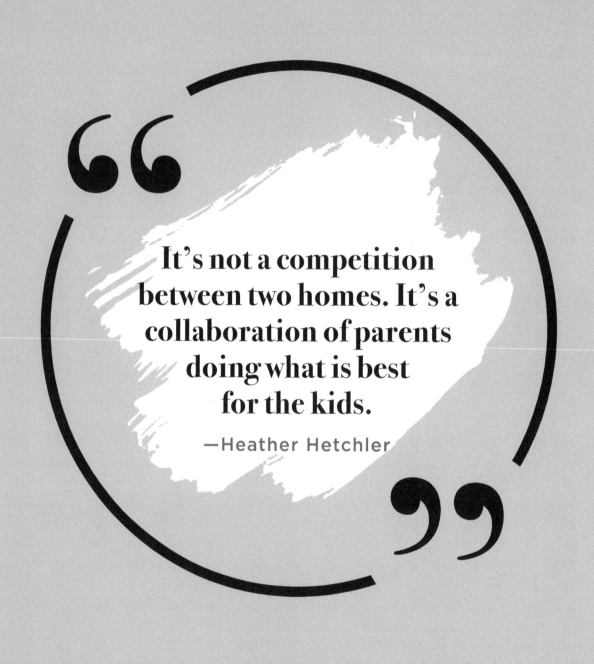

It's not a competition between two homes. It's a collaboration of parents doing what is best for the kids.

—Heather Hetchler

Dealing with a Difficult Co-Parent

AS MENTIONED IN the first section, a problematic parent may be wounded or broken. Because of those broken places, they may engage in behaviors that make things difficult for both you and your children. For example, they may be reluctant communicators or try to communicate through the children, putting them in the middle. In addition, they may attempt to make you look bad to the children or even undermine you. In the extreme, this behavior could be considered parental alienation. Many parents fail to understand, however, that in making the other parent look bad, they are causing more harm to the children than the other parent. A child's identity is determined by how they identify with both parents. If they see their other parent negatively, they will ultimately see themselves in a negative light and feel unsafe in the ongoing tension between parents.

The research is clear that children do well in low-conflict marriages and low-conflict divorces. On the other hand, children do not manage high conflict well in either marriage or divorce. When there is tension in the co-parenting relationship, children will feel it, even if they aren't old enough to articulate what they are experiencing. When dealing with a challenging co-parent, the most effective course of action is to reduce the conflict—not for the co-parent's sake, but for the emotional safety of the children. This section will offer ideas about setting boundaries and creating agreements to reduce ambiguity and create parameters for expectations.

What are your thoughts, fears, and goals at this point in your process?

_____

_____

_____

_____

_____

_____

_____

_____

_____

_____

_____

_____

_____

_____

_____

In what ways do I understand the broken parts of my partner? In what ways do I understand my broken parts? How might I be sensitive to any of these wounds?

_____

_____

_____

_____

_____

_____

_____

_____

_____

_____

_____

_____

_____

_____

When my co-parent triggers me, touching one of my sensitive areas, how can I be compassionate to that wounded part of me?

_____

_____

_____

_____

_____

_____

_____

_____

_____

_____

_____

_____

_____

_____

One way to protect sensitive areas is with good boundaries. What boundaries do I need to set for myself? Consider physical limits, boundaries around time and punctuality, and clarity concerning responsibilities.

_____

_____

_____

_____

_____

_____

_____

_____

_____

_____

_____

_____

_____

_____

_____

_____

_____

_____

_____

_____

_____

_____

_____

_____

_____

_____

_____

_____

_____

_____

_____

_____

_____

I'm creating a relationship with my former partner, honoring new co-parenting strategies. I feel good about the safety of limits that will be respectful and more businesslike. I am learning to notice my boundaries and those of my co-parent.

Seeing my co-parent in a more positive light requires me to honor my children by opening my heart. How have I stretched my perspective in ways that make me proud?

_____

_____

_____

_____

_____

_____

_____

_____

_____

_____

_____

_____

_____

_____

_____

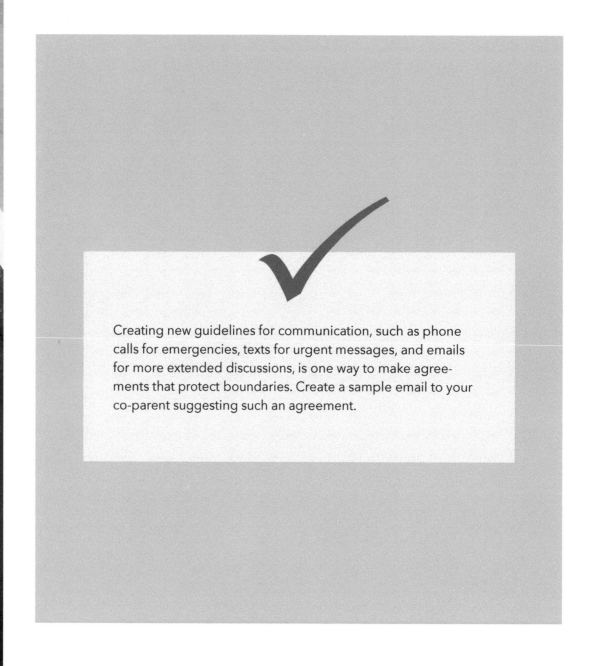

Creating new guidelines for communication, such as phone calls for emergencies, texts for urgent messages, and emails for more extended discussions, is one way to make agreements that protect boundaries. Create a sample email to your co-parent suggesting such an agreement.

If your co-parent was not the primary parent before, how will you accept that they will have a learning curve? Can you trust that your children will survive the mistakes?

_____

_____

_____

_____

_____

_____

_____

_____

_____

_____

_____

_____

_____

_____

I struggle to let go of controlling my child's experience with their other parent. Instead, I remember the experiences and skills I have offered them that will help them cope. What other resources can I provide?

_____

_____

_____

_____

_____

_____

_____

_____

_____

_____

_____

_____

_____

_____

_____

_____

_____

_____

_____

_____

_____

_____

_____

_____

_____

_____

_____

_____

_____

_____

_____

_____

_____

We may project our feelings about how we have been treated by our co-parent onto our children, imagining that they are experiencing the same. How might I be making these assumptions?

_____

_____

_____

_____

_____

_____

_____

_____

_____

_____

_____

_____

_____

_____

Incredible change happens in your life when you decide to take control of what you have power over instead of craving control over what you don't.

—Steve Maraboli

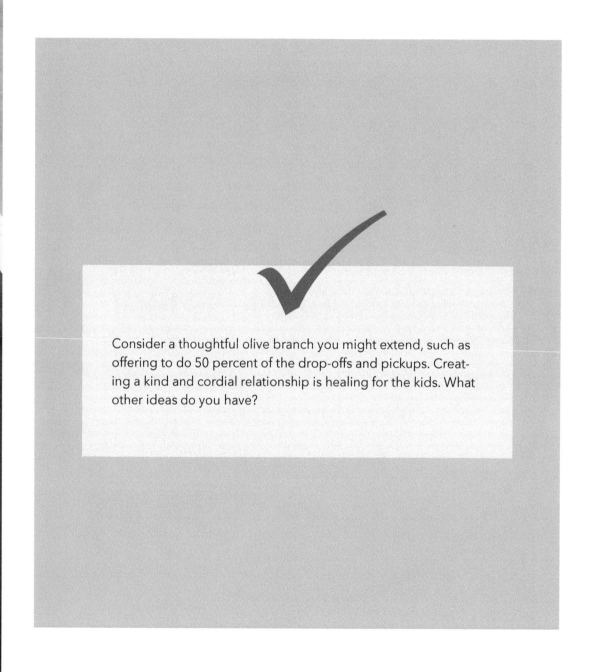

Consider a thoughtful olive branch you might extend, such as offering to do 50 percent of the drop-offs and pickups. Creating a kind and cordial relationship is healing for the kids. What other ideas do you have?

Create a script explaining the divorce to others in a way that would not put either parent in a negative light if the children were to hear it.

_____

_____

_____

_____

_____

_____

_____

_____

_____

_____

_____

_____

_____

_____

_____

How do I feel about my co-parent coming into my home when I'm not there? When I'm there? Are there circumstances in which this would be acceptable? Have I been clear about this?

_____

_____

_____

_____

_____

_____

_____

_____

_____

_____

_____

_____

_____

_____

What do I know about my child that is helpful to share with my co-parent? I want my children to know we communicate, and sharing this information may help their relationship.

_____

_____

_____

_____

_____

_____

_____

_____

_____

_____

_____

_____

_____

Many parents are unwilling to do the hard work of letting go of the marital relationship to have a good co-parenting relationship. However, I am doing this hard work for my children and feeling outstanding about myself as a parent.

Sometimes you find yourself completely exhausted and out of patience. This is a good reminder to stop and take care of yourself.

1. Lie down on the ground or a bed with your eyes closed.

2. Starting at the top of your head, tighten your forehead, release the muscles, and relax.

3. Do this with every muscle group descending to your toes.

4. When finished, scan your body to see where you might still hold tension. Repeat the tense-and-release in those areas.

5. Once completely relaxed, take a few deep breaths, noticing the ground or bed supporting your body.

When I work so hard as a parent, I may find myself reflecting on my childhood. Am I discovering wounds that may need healing despite my parents' best intentions?

_____

_____

_____

_____

_____

_____

_____

_____

_____

_____

_____

_____

_____

_____

Regardless of how my co-parent treats me, when my child is grown, what do I want them to remember about how I treated their other parent?

_____

_____

_____

_____

_____

_____

_____

_____

_____

_____

_____

_____

_____

_____

_____

Draft an email to your co-parent regarding transitions. Assume that your co-parent might be seeing the child struggle with changing households at their end as well. Share some of your observations and ask if they might be willing to do some brainstorming with you so that, as a team, you can better address the child's apparent struggles. Include an example of a change you are implementing on your end. Planting the seed that you are a team working together for your child may make your co-parent less defensive and build a foundation for future areas in which collaboration will be required to benefit your child.

When my child returns to me from being with their other parent, the transition can be difficult. What factors make this transition challenging, including some that are unrelated to my co-parent?

_____

_____

_____

_____

_____

_____

_____

_____

_____

_____

_____

_____

_____

_____

When I work so hard to keep the peace, it feels unfair. Although I know that divorce is not fair, sometimes I need to allow myself those feelings and to journal all my thoughts.

_____

_____

_____

_____

_____

_____

_____

_____

_____

_____

_____

_____

_____

_____

_____

_____

How can I keep refocusing on my child's needs and not make it about my negative feelings? Where can I let go and just be the best parent I can be?

_____

_____

_____

_____

_____

_____

_____

_____

_____

_____

_____

_____

_____

_____

_____

When my co-parent is disapproving of me, I may notice a lot of feelings emerge. Why is their opinion of me so vitally important? Am I giving them too much power?

_____

_____

_____

_____

_____

_____

_____

_____

_____

_____

_____

_____

_____

_____

_____

_____

_____

_____

_____

_____

_____

_____

_____

_____

_____

_____

_____

_____

_____

_____

_____

_____

_____

_____

_____

Friends and family often try to support me by fueling my anger. How can I gently remind them that I need their help to stay positively engaged with my co-parent?

_____

_____

_____

_____

_____

_____

_____

_____

_____

_____

_____

_____

_____

_____

Although we may see our co-parent's behavior as toxic, often we are seeing them through the lens of our hurt and anger. We may also worry about our inability to protect our children from an unwanted parenting style. Some behaviors, such as physical punishment, berating, abuse, and neglect, warrant professional intervention. In those situations, it's essential to seek co-parent counseling. If your co-parent is unwilling to attend with you, it may be time to consult a lawyer or involve protective services. Using a separate piece of paper, please list the behaviors that concern you. Then decide how you might gently approach your co-parent and invite them to attend co-parent counseling so that you can work together to benefit the children.

I am learning to respect and better understand my feelings. This way, I show kindness to myself and my co-parent. This work is arduous, and I deserve to be profoundly proud of who I have become and the work I continue to do.

Often when we get angry at our co-parent, underlying that anger is a deep sadness and disappointment at the many ways in which our or our children's needs were not met and dreams not realized. We may react with rage. The intensity of that anger is determined less by this one incident and more by the deep well of sadness. Make a list of the memories that repeatedly come up when you are feeling angry. Next to each item, note what you wished had happened and compassionately grieve that this was not the outcome. Then imagine this memory dissolving into the sea.

When I interact poorly with my co-parent, can I forgive myself with compassion and then apologize in the way I hope they would to me? If not, what gets in my way?

_____

_____

_____

_____

_____

_____

_____

_____

_____

_____

_____

_____

_____

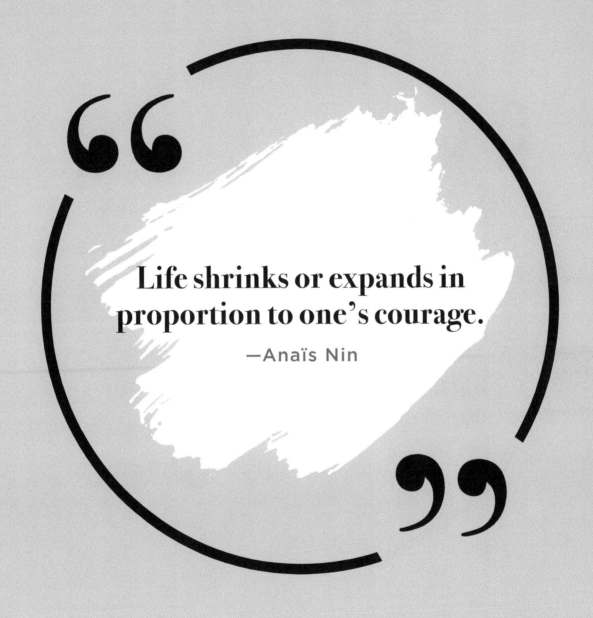

Life shrinks or expands in proportion to one's courage.

—Anaïs Nin

> "Our job as parents isn't to make our kids happy all the time. Our job is to prepare them for living fulfilling lives and we need resilience to face the daily challenges we're bound to meet.
>
> —Alissa Zorn

Helping Your Child Thrive

THIS SECTION IS about helping your children develop resilience during this difficult time and ultimately thrive. It will shift the focus from you and your co-parent to your child and how you can best support them. Divorce is likely to be the most challenging transition your child will experience. But, in actuality, divorce is not one transition for your child but rather a series of changes. Each change may build on the resolution of earlier challenges. If your child has not mastered an earlier challenge, old feelings could add to the emotional burden of the current challenge. Thus, each challenge is an opportunity for you to help your child work through any lingering feelings about earlier issues. One of the nice things about parenting is that we get second chances.

Children need to know they are safe and secure and will continue to be loved by both parents. They need to know they can talk with their parents about their concerns. You will help them see that they can express their feelings and safely ask questions. They need to know that their parents are all right emotionally and financially and do not need to be cared for so that they can continue to be children. They need to know that if their parents stopped loving each other, it doesn't mean they could ever stop loving them. They need to know that their parents will still communicate about them. Finally, they need to experience a low-conflict relationship between their parents.

When my child notices I am sad, I can explain it is okay for me to have feelings. How can I demonstrate to my child that I am taking care of myself?

_____

_____

_____

_____

_____

_____

_____

_____

_____

_____

_____

_____

_____

_____

When my child seems angry, it may be how they ask for reassurance or a chance to cry or talk. Write about this new lens through which we can consider their needs.

_____

_____

_____

_____

_____

_____

_____

_____

_____

_____

_____

_____

_____

_____

I may feel less overwhelmed by my child's questions if I consider possible questions and answers in advance. What might the questions be? What is appropriate for them to know?

_____

_____

_____

_____

_____

_____

_____

_____

_____

_____

_____

_____

_____

_____

_____

Given what you learned earlier in the book about children's need to see both parents in a favorable light, it will be essential for you to consider how you can authentically contribute to your child's positive views of their other parent. Although your marriage failed and you may have some lingering anger and sadness, if you breathe and stretch, you can still remember your co-parent's best qualities as a person and a parent. How do you want to help your child see these things so that they can also proudly see these qualities in themselves? Support this growing positive identity.

I am learning to make my needs secondary to my child's needs, even during an incredibly challenging time. As a result, I feel good about digging deep and making my love for my child into a verb: parenting at its best!

When my child is upset about their other parent's behavior, I will listen and help them figure out how to talk to their other parent about the concern. Here are examples of how they can do this.

_____

_____

_____

_____

_____

_____

_____

_____

_____

_____

_____

_____

_____

_____

_____

> **If we are to teach real peace in this world, and if we are to carry on a real war against war, we shall have to begin with the children.**
>
> —Mahatma Gandhi

When my child reports concerning co-parent behavior, how might I talk to my co-parent in a way that offers the benefit of the doubt and considers their version?

_____

_____

_____

_____

_____

_____

_____

_____

_____

_____

_____

_____

_____

_____

Make a list of all of your co-parent's behaviors that concern you. Put a check next to each behavior you might be able to change. Draw a plus sign next to each item checked that has an adverse impact on your child. Next to those items that have both a check and a plus, create a nonjudgmental narrative that you think you could share with your co-parent in a way they could hear. Prioritize those items so that you don't bombard your co-parent with perceived criticism or suggestions. Consider whether you could accept similar requests made of you.

What experience do I have with giving up control? How can I use that experience to help me let go of my need to change some of my co-parent's behaviors?

_____

_____

_____

_____

_____

_____

_____

_____

_____

_____

_____

_____

_____

_____

_____

_____

_____

_____

_____

_____

_____

_____

_____

_____

_____

_____

_____

_____

_____

_____

_____

_____

When my co-parent asks for a schedule change that allows my child to participate in a fun activity, how can I get past any irritation and consider more flexibility?

_____

_____

_____

_____

_____

_____

_____

_____

_____

_____

_____

_____

_____

_____

_____

If I will be unavailable during my scheduled parenting time, would I consider offering my co-parent that time with our child rather than hiring a babysitter? What are my thoughts?

_____

_____

_____

_____

_____

_____

_____

_____

_____

_____

_____

_____

_____

_____

_____

What agreements do I want to make with my co-parent about traveling with our child? What might best serve our child? Do we want to share itineraries and contact information?

_____

_____

_____

_____

_____

_____

_____

_____

_____

_____

_____

_____

_____

_____

Developing an understanding about introducing significant others to children is an important consideration. Children may quickly get attached to or struggle to accept a significant other. They may also fear that this person could replace them in that parent's heart. Many parents agree not to introduce anyone until they have been dating for six to nine months and believe this person will be in their life for a long time. Parents may also agree to allow the other parent to meet the significant other before introducing them to the child, so the child experiences openness. Consider how you might come to an agreement.

Learning that my co-parent is dating may stir up feelings for me. Is there anger, sadness, a sense of betrayal, rejection, relief, concern, or something else? What do I compassionately notice?

_____

_____

_____

_____

_____

_____

_____

_____

_____

_____

_____

_____

_____

_____

Do I fear that my co-parent's significant other will try to replace me as a parent? Do I understand that no one can take the spot I have in my child's heart?

_____

_____

_____

_____

_____

_____

_____

_____

_____

_____

_____

_____

_____

How can I help my child develop a good relationship with my co-parent's new significant other? How can I help them see that I am comfortable with this new person?

_____

_____

_____

_____

_____

_____

_____

_____

_____

_____

_____

_____

_____

_____

_____

Children are likely to complain to each parent about the other. Look for opportunities to make your child feel safe by not aligning with them in speaking badly about your co-parent. Part of their safe feeling is knowing you will remain united as parents, even as you are divorcing. Let them know you hear their concerns and believe their other parent loves them and wants to know how they feel. Help your child strategize what they might say to their other parent to address their concerns. Finally, make a kind call, text, or email to your co-parent to give them a heads-up.

How do I feel about my significant other disciplining my child? (Generally, this is a role that is reserved for parents unless the significant other gets permission to intervene in a specific situation.)

_____

_____

_____

_____

_____

_____

_____

_____

_____

_____

_____

_____

_____

_____

When my child is with their other parent, it's my time to refuel, which makes me a better parent. What feeds me? How do I want to spend this time?

_____

_____

_____

_____

_____

_____

_____

_____

_____

_____

_____

_____

_____

_____

_____

Dating again and becoming vulnerable is undoubtedly challenging. However, doing this while keeping my child the priority is an indication of my strength, clarity, and purpose. I may stumble, but I will always come back to prioritizing their needs.

There will always be things your co-parent does not like about your parenting. How will you discern when they are offering helpful feedback that you need to consider? How will you keep yourself from being defensive? Can you assume good intent just as you would want them to believe of you? It is more important for a child to experience consistency within households than between households. Is it harmful to your child if you are different in this way, or can they adapt? Can you and your co-parent agree to disagree? Write several versions of a respectful dialogue about parenting differences.

It is crucial that children feel secure. They need to know that nothing will change our love for them. So how can I show them my love is dependable?

_____

_____

_____

_____

_____

_____

_____

_____

_____

_____

_____

_____

_____

_____

_____

_____

_____

_____

_____

_____

_____

_____

_____

_____

_____

_____

_____

_____

_____

_____

What changes am I observing in my child? Am I accurately attributing them to the divorce, or is there an alternative explanation? How might I explore these changes with my child?

_____

_____

_____

_____

_____

_____

_____

_____

_____

_____

_____

_____

_____

_____

_____

_____

_____

_____

_____

_____

_____

_____

_____

_____

_____

_____

_____

_____

_____

_____

_____

_____

_____

_____

_____

When my child returns from their other home, I notice they are different and I want to help them with the transition. How can I best give them what they need?

_____

_____

_____

_____

_____

_____

_____

_____

_____

_____

_____

_____

_____

_____

Compose the song your child would sing about the divorce. What would the lyrics be? Would they feel loved? Would they feel confused and scared? What might those fears be? Would there be things about their new life that excite them? Would they feel safe in both households and know what to expect? Would they understand that the expectations of them have not changed? Might they be excited about having even more people in their life who love them? Would they be uncomfortable in either of their homes? What would the melody of this song be? Can it be a duet?

I give myself kudos for putting my child's needs before my desire for emotional satisfaction. Instead, I choose to support their relationship with their other parent. That choice is a sign of my love, maturity, and strength.

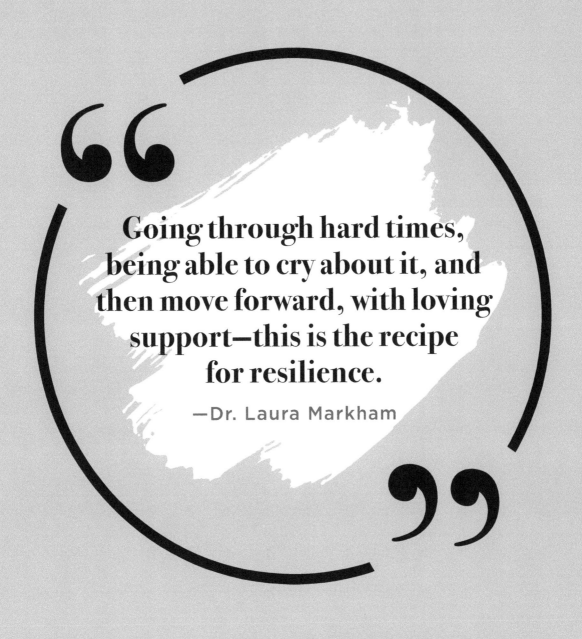

"

Going through hard times, being able to cry about it, and then move forward, with loving support—this is the recipe for resilience.

—Dr. Laura Markham

"

Have I considered involving professionals like my child's teacher or a child therapist? Sometimes a child will reveal more about their concerns to other people if they want to protect you.

_____

_____

_____

_____

_____

_____

_____

_____

_____

_____

_____

_____

_____

Every moment is a fresh beginning.

—T. S. Eliot

Healing Yourself

THE TRANSITIONS FROM marriage to separation, divorce to co-parenting, and beyond are not a sprint but a marathon. They can be exhausting, and it requires remarkable compassion to stay fueled. Frequent reminders about the importance of process and not perfection seem to be lubrication for getting through the hard times. Leaning into the questions with self-reflection and communication is a much stronger position than having immediate answers.

Perhaps one of the greatest gifts of growth that can come out of this evolution is humility. Humility is learning how very human we are and accepting that we have made many mistakes and will likely continue to do so. Mistakes are not an indication of failure but an opportunity for insight, growth, and a deeper understanding of ourselves, our co-parent, and our children.

Healing comes from self-compassion, self-acceptance, and humility, and from learning to live from a place of curiosity rather than judgment. When we judge ourselves and others, it is generally a shortcut we have learned to take to protect ourselves. Unfortunately, it is usually not effective. We are safer if we suspend judgment so that we can be curious and discover more profound truths.

Finally, healing is also about having fun. It is making time to rediscover what makes us laugh, and it helps us connect with others, brings meaning and satisfaction to our lives, and helps us feel good about ourselves and the world. Divorce is a time to grow into wholeness.

What do I value about myself as a co-parent, parent, and human being? I want to remember these qualities and stay true to who I am at my core.

_____

_____

_____

_____

_____

_____

_____

_____

_____

_____

_____

_____

_____

_____

_____

_____

What cues does my body offer me that I am tired or irritated and need a break? What gets in the way of my listening to my body?

_____

_____

_____

_____

_____

_____

_____

_____

_____

_____

_____

_____

_____

_____

During the healing process, we will invariably get triggered at times. When we get triggered, we often feel ungrounded. We may forget who we are and where we are, losing all sense of perspective and safety. Practice the following exercise for recentering yourself:

1. Look around the room and name five things that are your favorite color, such as green, red, orange, or blue.

2. Take a deep, slow inhale to the count of four, pause to the count of two, and slowly exhale to the count of six. Repeat.

3. Close your eyes and imagine you are in your most relaxing space, recalling the safety of that place.

When I regret a decision I made in my marriage or even the decision to get a divorce, what do I need to remember to find more self-compassion in my analysis?

_____

_____

_____

_____

_____

_____

_____

_____

_____

_____

_____

_____

_____

_____

You will inevitably make mistakes as a co-parent. For example, you will get triggered by things your co-parent does. When you are upset, you may become reactive and respond in a manner that is not helpful to your co-parenting relationship. Now is the time to write about the things that trigger you. Is there a pattern? Do these triggers give you information about the places inside you that need healing? What do you need to say to those hurt parts of yourself? For example, now that you are divorced, can you give your co-parent less power to upset you?

I love that I am learning to embrace my imperfections and love myself as I am. Not only does this change the way I see myself, but it also offers a model I want my children to adopt for themselves.

Sometimes I feel irritated with my co-parent because they are co-parenting in a way that feels less than perfect to me. How can I reframe my perspective to be more flexible?

_____

_____

_____

_____

_____

_____

_____

_____

_____

_____

_____

_____

_____

_____

If I forgive my co-parent for real or perceived transgressions, it will lighten my load and allow me to feel less constricted. Which things can I let go of now?

_____

_____

_____

_____

_____

_____

_____

_____

_____

_____

_____

_____

_____

_____

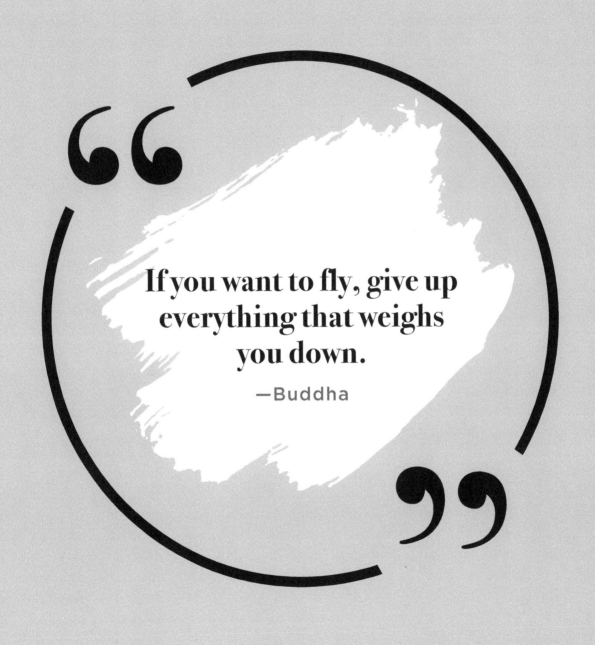

If you want to fly, give up everything that weighs you down.

—Buddha

Sometimes we hold on to anger and resentment as a way to protect ourselves from getting hurt again. But, as they say in Eastern philosophy, this is like holding on to a lump of hot coal and expecting the other person to get burned. Although the intent is understandable, in practice, these efforts are often ineffective and serve to hurt us more. When it happens, we can stop and recognize that they just don't have that kind of power anymore. Create a list of the things you are angry about and cross out those things that it is now time to release.

As I let go of some of my anger, what differences am I noticing about how my body feels? Where do I feel the change? How is it different?

_____

_____

_____

_____

_____

_____

_____

_____

_____

_____

_____

_____

_____

_____

Children have excellent radar for our feelings. Are my children observing my interactions with their other parent and aware that I am carrying less anger? What am I teaching them?

_____

_____

_____

_____

_____

_____

_____

_____

_____

_____

_____

_____

_____

_____

One reason I chose to leave my marriage was to offer my child a better model for healthy interactions. I feel so good about doing that now, as I am increasingly capable of showing up as my best self.

I have changed a lot since the last time I was single. What is different now about me? What is life calling me to do?

_____

_____

_____

_____

_____

_____

_____

_____

_____

_____

_____

_____

_____

_____

_____

Create a drawing or collage that depicts where you are in the healing process. Allow yourself to draw without a plan, letting any feelings and content emerge organically. What are the feelings you notice as you draw? Often feelings will arise that surprise us. Don't judge what develops on the paper or in your heart. Are there thoughts or memories that surprise you? Do you notice that you are critical of what enters your awareness? This drawing experience is an opportunity to be curious and gather information without judgment.

To build on the previous exercise, create a drawing with your nondominant hand. Research suggests that when we draw or write with our nondominant hand, we are more likely to experience unconscious feelings and thoughts coming to the surface. Notice how this experience may be different from the one you had when you did this exercise with your dominant hand on the previous page. Write about the things that came up that might be surprising to you. You might write with both hands about what emerged. Is there a difference when you write with different hands? Can you embrace both as different versions of your truth?

I miss my children when they are not with me, but I know this is my time to take care of myself. How do I want to spend my time?

_____

_____

_____

_____

_____

_____

_____

_____

_____

_____

_____

_____

_____

_____

_____

Everyone heals at a different rate. How will I respect my timeline and know when it might be time to start dating again? How will I know when I am whole?

_____

_____

_____

_____

_____

_____

_____

_____

_____

_____

_____

_____

_____

_____

_____

_____

If I begin to date, what are the qualities I am looking for in another person? What are the red flags I want to watch out for in this person?

_____

_____

_____

_____

_____

_____

_____

_____

_____

_____

_____

_____

_____

_____

Some of my friendships have changed since my divorce. What are the qualities I am looking for in friendships? What do I offer as a friend?

_____

_____

_____

_____

_____

_____

_____

_____

_____

_____

_____

_____

_____

_____

Sometimes during challenging transitions, and especially when we are newly single, we may find ourselves using substances or behaviors such as compulsive gambling or use of social media in a way that may not be healthy. What do I notice about my own substance use or addictive behaviors?

_____

_____

_____

_____

_____

_____

_____

_____

_____

_____

_____

_____

_____

_____

So much has changed not only in your life, but also within you. Who is this person you are becoming? Which changes are you enjoying, and which do you want to tweak? What wisdom have you accrued in this process? How have you changed as a parent? Are you still acting like a parent, or have you become more of a friend to your child? Knowing that children need parents no matter how old they are, do you need to look at that? How has your parenting improved?

Even when we choose to end a relationship, there is grief for the loss of the marriage and the dreams that did not materialize. What do I continue to grieve?

_____

_____

_____

_____

_____

_____

_____

_____

_____

_____

_____

_____

_____

_____

_____

Children going through a divorce may act out their feelings. I know this, but I still lose my temper from time to time. Am I able to forgive myself and apologize to them?

_____

_____

_____

_____

_____

_____

_____

_____

_____

_____

_____

_____

_____

_____

When I apologize to my child, am I able to do so with enough ease that my child learns it is okay to make mistakes, learn from them, and move on?

_____

_____

_____

_____

_____

_____

_____

_____

_____

_____

_____

_____

_____

_____

When my co-parent struggles in their relationship with our child, am I able to support them in a manner that contributes to resolution and growth in their relationship?

_____

_____

_____

_____

_____

_____

_____

_____

_____

_____

_____

_____

_____

_____

If we are lucky, life is a continuous process of growth. As I move through the healing of this chapter in my life, what do I want my future growth to be?

_____

_____

_____

_____

_____

_____

_____

_____

_____

_____

_____

_____

_____

_____

_____

_____

_____

_____

_____

_____

_____

_____

_____

_____

_____

_____

_____

_____

_____

_____

_____

_____

_____

_____

Co-parenting is almost always tricky, particularly with a challenging co-parent. Nevertheless, I am doing an excellent job for the sake of my child and deserve to feel proud of the sacrifices I make in the process. I am healing and growing.

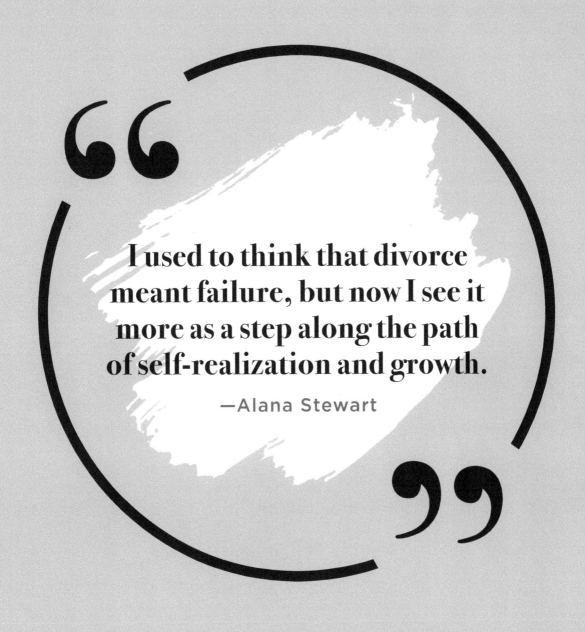

I used to think that divorce meant failure, but now I see it more as a step along the path of self-realization and growth.

—Alana Stewart

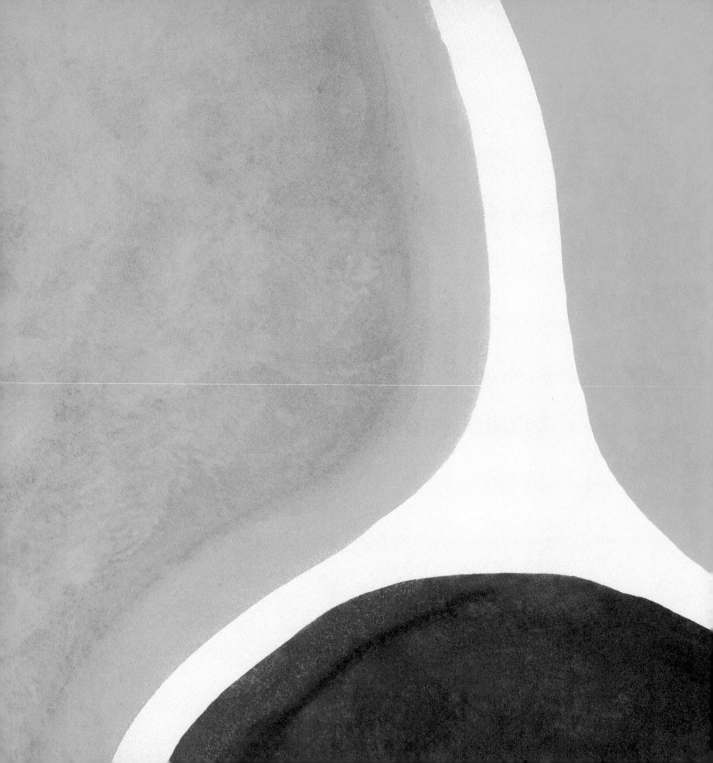

RESOURCES

Books for Parents

Broken Open: How Difficult Times Can Help Us Grow by Elizabeth Lesser

The Co-Parenting Handbook: Raising Well-Adjusted and Resilient Kids from Little Ones to Young Adults Through Divorce or Separation by Karen Bonell

Mindful Co-parenting: A Child-Friendly Path Through Divorce by Jeremy S. Gaies, PsyD

Mom's House, Dad's House: Making Two Homes for Your Child by Isolina Ricci, PhD

Radical Acceptance: Embracing Your Life with the Heart of a Buddha by Tara Brach

No Time Like the Present by Jack Kornfield

When Things Fall Apart by Pema Chodron

Hardwiring Happiness by Rick Hanson

Rising Strong: How the Ability to Reset Transforms the Way We Live, Love, Parent, and Lead by Brené Brown

Self-Compassion by Kristin Neff, PhD

Books for Children

Dinosaurs Divorce: A Guide for Changing Families by Marc Brown and Laurene Krasny Brown

Divorce Is the Worst by Anastasia Higginbotham

Was It the Chocolate Pudding?: A Story for Little Kids About Divorce by Sandra Levins and Bryan Langdo

Websites for Mindfulness

www.tarabrach.com

jackkornfield.com

www.rickhanson.net

Acknowledgments

There is no way to adequately acknowledge the many people who brought what I needed to write this book. The first, of course, are my children, who tolerated the many mistakes I made through divorce and co-parenting and loved me anyway. The second are the professionals at International Academy of Collaborative Professionals, who taught me a better way to divorce and co-parent. The third are the many individual clients and families who trusted me with their struggles and taught me volumes. Finally, there are the extraordinary women who sang my song to me until I could remember the tune, and the remarkable man who became my husband when all this was behind me and taught me what love could be.

About the Author

Susan Buniva, MSW, is a therapist in private practice in Richmond, Virginia. She is trained as a collaborative law divorce coach. In her practice, she sees individuals and couples for psychotherapy, collaborative law divorce coaching, co-parenting, and blended family therapy, and provides consultation to other therapists. When not engaged in these pursuits, she enjoys spending time with her husband, children, stepchildren, grandchildren, and dog, and the special friends who help keep her sane.

CPSIA information can be obtained
at www.ICGtesting.com
Printed in the USA
JSHW011236121221
21146JS00001B/1